DATE DUE

OCT 3 1990			

DEMCO 38-297

Chicago

★ GREAT ★ CITIES ★ OF THE ★ USA ★

☆ ☆ ☆

LIBRARY OF CONGRESS CATALOGING-IN-PUBLICATION DATA

Stewart, Gail, 1949-
    Chicago / by Gail Stewart.
      p. cm. -- (Great Cities of the United States)
    Includes index.
    Summary: An introduction to the history, economy, people, and notable sites of the city considered to be the leading industrial and transportation center of the United States.
    ISBN 0-86592-538-0
    1. Chicago (Ill.)--Description--1981- --Guide-books--Juvenile literature.
[1. Chicago (Ill.)--Description--Guides.] I. Title. II. Series: Stewart, Gail, 1949- Great Cities of the United States.
F548.33.S82 1989
917.73'110443--dc20   89-32409
                                                             CIP
                                                                AC

© 1989 Rourke Enterprises, Inc.

☆ ☆ ☆

Chicago

★ GREAT ★ CITIES ★ OF THE ★ USA ★

TEXT BY
GAIL STEWART

DESIGN & PRODUCTION BY
MARK E. AHLSTROM
(The Bookworks)

**ROURKE
ENTERPRISES,
INC.**
Vero Beach, FL 32964
U.S.A.

A City
On the Move...

☆ ☆ ☆

977.3
5

TABLE OF CONTENTS

CREDITS

All Photos: FPG International

Peter Gridley .... cover photo, 4

Cezus 7, 12, 27, 30, 31

FPG 11

Photoworld 14, 15, 16

Lee Balterman 17, 29, 33, 42

Keystone View Co./Photoworld 18-19

Karl Fliehler 21

Fredric Stein 22, 28, 40-41

Jim Pickerell 23

David J. Maenza 24, 32

J. Blank 34, 43

Al Michaud 35

Lee Foster 37

William Cramp 38-39

TYPESETTING AND LAYOUT: THE FINAL WORD
PRINTING: WORZALLA PUBLISHING CO.

143342

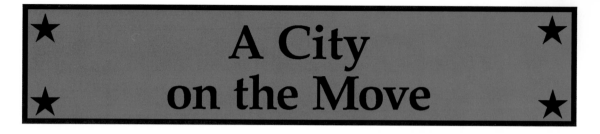

A City on the Move

Carl Sandburg wrote a poem about Chicago in 1918. A Chicagoan himself, Sandburg was proud of his hometown. He was aware that Chicago wasn't like other big cities. It was not known for its elegant fashions and high society, as were New York and Paris. It was certainly not known for its sunny climate, as were Miami and Los Angeles.

What Chicago **was** known for, in Carl Sandburg's time, was its sheer size and strength. Chicago was the site of the world's largest stockyards—more cattle, sheep, and hogs were butchered there than in any other place in the world. Chicago was a leader in heavy industries such as tool making and machinery. It was, and is today, the busiest railroad center in the United States. Its biggest airport, O'Hare, is the busiest in the world. Flights take off or land every 11 seconds!

In his poem, Sandburg called Chicago "Hog Butcher for the World" and "City of the Big Shoulders." No other city could match Chicago in muscle and might. So what if it wasn't a cultural center like New York, with lovely theaters, symphony orchestras, and ballet? Chicago was just fine the way it was—a little rough around the edges, maybe, but a city always moving, always working.

Some things about Chicago have certainly changed in the more than 70 years since Sandburg wrote his Chicago poem. The big stockyards are gone—they were moved to Kansas and Missouri. Some of the areas that were used for railroad yards are now occupied by apartment buildings and condominiums. The Computer Age has meant the end of much heavy industry. New, light industry has replaced many of the old machinery factories of Sandburg's day.

Chicago, the metropolis in the heart of the nation, prides itself on being a little rough around the edges. The city's name comes from an Indian word that means "onion swamp."

Yet there are many things about Chicago that are the same now as they were for Carl Sandburg. Chicago is still a city of planning and building and rebuilding. Old buildings fall under the wrecking ball, while new buildings are constantly being constructed.

Although it now boasts great theaters and museums, Chicagoans still pride themselves on being a little rough around the edges. They are proud that they are part of a working, changing city. Chicago, they say, is still a city on the move.

CHICAGO THEN AND NOW

The area in northeast Illinois that is now Chicago was inhabited by Native Americans thousands of years ago. The Potawatomi tribe had a settlement on the swampy section of land near Lake Michigan. Their village was close to a river they called *Chikagou*. That's where the word "Chicago" comes from. *Chikagou* in the Potawatomi language meant "onion swamp." They must have named the river because of the strong-smelling wild onion plants that grew along the banks of the river.

The first non-Indian visitors to the area came in 1673. They were the French-Canadian explorers Louis Joliet and Jacques Marquette. The Potawatomis were helpful in showing the explorers the way to portage, or carry, their canoe between the Chikagou River and the Des Plaines River. The Des Plaines connected with the Illinois River, which in turn connected with the Mississippi River. By portaging, travelers could get from the shores of Lake Michigan all the way down to the Gulf of Mexico!

It was in the 1770's that a black fur trader named Jean Baptiste Point du Sable came to the area from New Orleans. Du Sable was a good businessman, and his trading with the Indians was very profitable. He built a log cabin on the banks of the Chikagou. For 30 years du Sable's business grew and prospered. Because his cabin was the first non-Indian structure built in the area, du Sable is considered the founder of Chicago.

Fort Dearborn

Du Sable sold his business in 1800. There were many new people to take his place. Settlers from the East were moving to Illinois, having heard about the prairies and good farmland. They feared the Indians who lived nearby, however, and rightly so.

Many of the Indians had been cruelly treated by the U.S. government—often forced to give away their land for almost nothing in return. Several tribes were angry, and vowed revenge on these newcomers who wanted to steal what belonged to the Indians. Attacks on unprotected settlements were becoming common.

To protect the settlers, the government built a fort with high walls. Soldiers would be close by in case of trouble, and families could hurry inside the walls of the fort if there was danger. Fort Dearborn was built very close to du Sable's log cabin on the Chikagou.

For a time there was no trouble at all. But in 1812, the United States was involved in a war with the British. The British persuaded many Indian tribes to attack American settlements. The Potawatomis were one of those tribes.

In August of 1812, it was decided that Fort Dearborn wasn't strong enough to handle a major attack. The soldiers and civilians nearby were urged to move to Fort Wayne, in Indiana. Less than a mile from Fort Dearborn, the group of 110 men, women, and children was attacked by 500 Potawatomi fighting men. The "battle" was over in less than 15 minutes. Half of the soldiers and settlers were killed, while the rest were taken prisoner. Fort Dearborn was burned to the ground.

From Settlement to City

More than four years passed before settlers felt brave enough to return to the area. Fort Dearborn was rebuilt in 1816, and slowly but steadily more people came. In 1833 "Chicago," as the area was now known, was incorporated as a village. Fewer than 150 people lived there.

But again, government officials were pressuring the Indians to sell their land. The Potawatomis were forced to sell in 1835. Many of these

Indians went to live on reservations in Kansas.

It seemed that the departure of the Indians was what many of the more timid settlers had been waiting for. Two years after the Potawatomis were forced out, the population of Chicago was more than 4,000! Chicago was incorporated as a full-fledged city in 1837.

For a couple of important reasons, it seemed that the young city would never stop growing. Shipping canals were built in 1848. These canals followed the old Indian canoe portage—they linked the Chicago River with the Mississippi River. Soon the city was booming with trade from all over the United States.

Another important reason for Chicago's fast growth was its railroad systems. The city was a center of railroad lines—from the South, the East, and the West. More than 100 trains arrived or departed every day. Chicago had become home for eleven railroad companies by 1857. Thousands of miles of track crisscrossed the city.

Many of the incoming trains were packed with immigrants from European countries, coming to find a new way of life in this growing town. Thousands of factories were thriving in the city. Huge, modern stockyards were built to keep the millions of animals brought in to be slaughtered by the packing companies. From the Western states would come railroad cars loaded with cattle and pigs. After being butchered, out the meat would go in special cars to cities in the East and the South.

Business was booming, and Chicago was booming right along with it.

Blaming the Cow

By 1871, the city's population had swelled to 300,000. Most of those people lived in wooden houses built very close together. Factories, churches, and businesses were all made of wood. Because the roads of Chicago were always so muddy (remember, the city was built on a swamp!) there were even wood ramps used as sidewalks and streets.

With all of this wood, together

The Great Chicago Fire of 1871 forced thousands of panic-stricken people to run from the flames. The fire burned for three days, killed 300 people, and left more than 100,000 homeless.

with a hot dry summer, it isn't hard to understand how a fire could be a very dangerous thing. On October 8, 1871, that's just what happened!

The fire began on the west side of Chicago, in a barn belonging to the O'Leary family. Legend says that the O'Leary's cow kicked a lantern over, but Mrs. O'Leary denied that. Whatever the actual cause was, the fire spread quickly. High, gusty winds showered sparks across the river to the south side, and then downtown.

Fire fighters trying to contain the blaze realized that they were no match for the winds and intense heat. Thousands and thousands of people fled from their homes, grabbing a few belongings and running east, toward Lake Michigan. Many were forced by the intense, scorching heat to wade up to their necks in the cold water.

The fire burned for three days. At

The Water Tower survived the Great Chicago Fire. It is now a landmark in the heart of downtown Chicago on a part of Michigan Avenue called "The Magnificent Mile."

the end of that time, 300 people were dead. More than 100,000 people were without homes. Three-and-one-half square miles of city had burned to the ground. One witness to the fire said the destruction was so great that you could see a friend standing among the flattened ruins three miles away!

The Great Chicago Fire, as it is now called, was one of the worst disasters in the history of our country. At the time it seemed that the city was lost forever. The fire had destroyed the buildings, the businesses, even the streets. There were no means of transportation—even if the streets hadn't been so choked with rubble, there was no place to go.

There were no police or fire stations, no banks, no food or water. Very little was left. But the people of Chicago felt that they could rebuild. Joseph Medill, then the publisher of the Chicago *Tribune* newspaper, vowed that "Chicago would rise again."

If ever a city had the energy and muscle to begin again, it was Chicago.

The Second City, and Beyond

Within a few days, some businesses and banks reopened—many of them operating out of little shacks. Food and blankets were handed out by emergency teams, and many people set to work building new homes. This time, most of the structures would be brick and stone, rather than the wood that had proved so dangerous.

Architects, people who design new buildings, were called in to help plan the "second" Chicago. Famous architects like Louis Sullivan, William Le Baron Jenney, and Daniel H. Burnham were excited about trying out new ideas. In fact, it was in Chicago that the first steel-framed skyscraper was built in 1885. By using steel and concrete and avoiding heavy brick and stone, builders could erect taller, more modern-looking buildings.

Chicago became a showplace— proof of what a city on the move could become. Once again, business was booming. Industries were doing well, and railroads were working even more efficiently than before.

The early years of the 20th century brought expansion and growth in many ways. By 1900, the population of Chicago had ballooned to over a million people—making Chicago the second largest city in the nation, behind New York City. Many of these people were immigrants from Poland, Ireland, Yugoslavia, and Italy. Thousands of blacks moved to Chicago from the South, hoping to get away from racial problems. Many of these people found jobs in Chicago's factories.

Growing Pains

The 1920's were a time of big problems for Chicago. Congress had passed a law saying that the making, selling, and drinking of liquor was illegal in the United States. Many people were angry about this law, and continued to drink illegally.

By the 1930's, Chicago had 10 lanes of traffic on the Inner Drive near Lake Michigan.

Alcoholic drinks were made and distributed to people, even though it was against the law. This time was called Prohibition.

Some criminals came to Chicago from New York and took over the illegal sale, called bootlegging, of liquor. They also controlled many other kinds of crime in the city, such as gambling and bribing government officials. One of the most notorious of the criminals was "Scarface" Al Capone. Capone and his gang terror-ized Chicago for many years during the time of Prohibition.

Chicago earned the reputation of being a violent, wild town. In some ways the reputation was deserved. Historians say, for example, that so many gangland shootings took place on the North Side of Chicago, near the streets of Oak and Cambridge, that the intersection there was known as "Death Corner."

Chicago got through the violence and crime of the 1920's and '30's,

A March snowstorm in 1931 stopped traffic, like this streetcar, throughout the city. It took 20,000 men to clear the snow from the streets.

but the city's problems weren't over. The hundreds of thousands of immigrants streaming into the city were in need of housing. Schools were overcrowded and understaffed. Transportation systems were clogged and slow. Schools never seemed to have enough money to do the job that needed to be done.

Many of the problems that plagued Chicago in the mid-1900's are still problems today. But many Chicagoans are trying to help their city. They know that to turn things around they must be actively concerned about Chicago. They know that people working together is one of the best ways to solve problems.

"Sometimes it's easy to forget that it's people who are the most important part of the city," said one Chicago official. "Hundred-story

Chicago gangster Al "Scarface" Capone (hand to chin) occupied a front-row seat at a 1931 football game. Two days later, he was tried on charges of income tax evasion.

skyscrapers and busy airports are interesting, but they're only there to serve Chicago's most valuable asset. Don't ever underestimate Chicagoans, they'll fool you every time.

"Problems? Sure, we've got lots of them. But any town that can rebuild so fast from one of the worst fires in history can do anything!"

Thousands of runners fill the streets as they compete in a marathon. Chicagoans—and their energy—are the city's most valuable asset.

Bumper-to-bumper traffic on Michigan Avenue was not uncommon even in the early part of the 20th century.

To really understand a city, it's important to see how it is laid out. Where do the people work? Where do they live? What are the neighborhoods like?

Chicago stretches 25 miles along the shore of Lake Michigan. The city takes up almost 230 square miles. Although it used to be second only to New York in terms of size, Chicago is officially now third—behind Los Angeles.

Besides the downtown area, where most of the large office buildings and skyscrapers are, Chicago includes the North Side, South Side, and West Side. There is no East Side—that's where Lake Michigan is. Chicago's more than three million citizens live in various neighborhoods around the city. Each neighborhood, any Chicagoan will tell you, has a personality and flavor all its own.

Downtown

Probably the first section of the downtown area that a visitor learns about is called the Loop, just south of the Chicago River. The Loop is so named because of the "loop" of elevated train tracks that circle the area. The elevated trains, called "the Els," make frequent, noisy runs between downtown and the suburbs that ring the city.

In addition to the Els, Chicagoans rely on buses and commuter trains to take them from their homes to various parts of the city. The Burlington Northern Railroad, for example, makes frequent express runs from downtown to the outlying suburbs, and back again, every day. This saves money not only on gas but also on parking fees, which are quite expensive in downtown Chicago!

The Loop is a busy, bustling place.

Visitors to the city are almost always amazed at the number of elegant buildings in the Loop—some old, some quite new. Chicago's Loop has been called a showplace of 20th century architecture.

One of the most famous buildings is the Carson Pirie Scott store on State and Madison Streets. Built in 1899 by the noted architect Louis Sullivan, the Carson building has a beautiful curved "corner," called a rotunda. There are interesting metal and wood ornaments on the building, too, that make it one of the most photographed in the city.

The John Hancock Building is another famous structure in downtown Chicago. "Big John," as Chicagoans have nicknamed the building, is a modern building, made of black glass and steel girders. It is a strong, forceful structure, easily recognizable in the Chicago skyline.

Lake Point Towers, designed by architect Mies van der Rohe, are as graceful as the Hancock is strong. The Towers are like a three-dimen-

The John Hancock Center (tall, dark building with twin towers) is nicknamed "Big John." It was the tallest building in Chicago until the Sears Tower was built.

Residents of Lake Point Towers get a bird's-eye view of Navy Pier and Lake Michigan. Architect Mies van der Rohe designed the curved building.

sional wave of curved glass—one would be hard-pressed to find a sharp corner anywhere!

La Salle Street in the Loop is the financial district of Chicago. Many banks are there, in addition to the Chicago Board of Trade and the Midwest Stock Exchange.

The tallest building in the world stands in Chicago's Loop. The Sears Tower, all 1,454 feet of it, rises 110 stories above the streets below!

North of the Chicago River, just beyond the Loop, is one of Chicago's dearest landmarks—the Water Tower. The Water Tower is one of the few structures that escaped the flames of the Chicago Fire in 1871. An ultra-modern collection of shops, restaurants, hotels, and businesses now exists near the old tower on a part of Michigan Avenue that is called "The Magnificent Mile."

It's important to remember, too,

The Sears Tower, 110 stories high, is the tallest building in the world. Its 1,454 feet rise above the other skyscrapers of The Loop, Chicago's business district.

Michigan Avenue is the site of many shops, restaurants, hotels, and businesses. The Water Tower (on the left), which survived the Great Chicago Fire of 1871, offers a contrast to the ultra-modern buildings.

that downtown Chicago isn't only for businesses. Many people live downtown. More than 33,000 people occupy elegant high rises, some of which look out over Lake Michigan. What a view!

From the Gold Coast to Cabrini-Green— the North Side

In the far northwest part of the North Side is O'Hare Airport, the busiest and most modern airport in the country. Aside from the airport area, however, the city's North Side is almost completely residential.

If Chicago is a city of contrasts, then the North Side is no exception. More than 1.5 million people live on the North Side. Some are surrounded by luxury and wealth; others struggle to survive. As one Chicagoan remarked, "Never have heaven and hell stood so close together."

"Heaven" would certainly include the Gold Coast, a beautiful area of mansions, lovely old apartment buildings, and world-class high-rise apartments. The Gold Coast is a good name for the place, one writer jokes, because it costs a fortune to live there. The Gold Coast is tucked between Lincoln Park and the glitzy Magnificent Mile.

Nearby is the elegant Carl Sandburg Village. More than 7,000 people, most of them single, young, and prosperous, live in the village. Its residents are pleased with its closeness to downtown offices and shops.

Just a few blocks from the cheerful atmosphere of the Gold Coast and the Village is a stark reminder of how bad poverty can be. It is the area of the North Side known as Cabrini-Green. From a distance the shape of the tall buildings resembles the high-rises of the Carl Sandburg Village, but a second look will show glaring differences.

Cabrini-Green is a housing project designed for poor people. Most of the project's 15,000 residents are black. Most are frightened to walk out of their apartments. Crime and drug pushers are everywhere around Cabrini-Green.

Garbage lies in heaps around the buildings, both inside and out. Bullet holes in windows and walls indicate that it is a violent place. Indeed, say Chicago officials, it is one of the most dangerous places in all of America. According to police records, someone gets shot there every other day during the summer—many of them innocent bystanders caught in the crossfire of the warring gangs.

Taxicabs won't pick up or deliver people to Cabrini-Green. Sometimes ambulances and fire trucks are shot at or attacked, so they often stay away, too. Many who live in Cabrini-Green ask themselves if they will ever feel safe.

One mother shakes her head and says, "I lost my hope the day my five-year-old stopped asking about the gunshots he hears all the time. He just accepts the fact that people are getting killed outside every day."

The South Side

The South Side, too, is a mixture of pleasant communities, interesting shops and businesses, and pockets of real poverty. In all, about 1.5 million people live there.

Chinatown is located on the South Side. Most of its 7,000 people speak no English. They feel very much apart from the city government. They have neighborhood councils (all meetings conducted in Chinese) and have made the area truly their own. Visitors come to Chinatown because of the excellent restaurants and places to shop.

One of the most famous neighborhoods on the South Side is Bridgeport. Between 1933 and 1979, every Chicago mayor came from Bridgeport! You might think it is a wealthy area whose residents are lawyers and judges, but that's not the case.

Bridgeport is a very modest little area of small, clean cottages. The first people to live in Bridgeport were the Irish immigrants who came to Chicago to help build the canals in 1848. They established churches, businesses, and schools there, and became very active in political life. Virtually all of them were Democrats—and more than a couple of

Lakeshore Drive runs to the South Side along Lake Michigan.

them became mayors!

Now Bridgeport is part Irish, and part Polish. Visitors like to visit the neighborhood because it seems like a small town, cut off from the rest of the city.

"Back of the Yards" seems like a strange name for a neighborhood. It gets its name from Chicago's Union Stockyards, which, until they closed down in 1971, were the largest and busiest in the world. The air in Back of the Yards stank. It was almost too foul to breathe. But the people who lived around the "yards" had no other choices. They were mostly Polish people, and very poor. They worked in the slaughterhouses and the packing plants.

The air is cleaner now, and the neighborhood is different. There are as many Spanish-speaking people as Poles. The Back of the Yarders have organized a strong neighborhood

The Rockefeller Memorial Chapel (in foreground) is a center of religious life at the University of Chicago. The University is in the heart of the South Side.

council that is trying very hard to fight drugs and gangs. They want Back of the Yards to be a good place to raise their families.

Needing Help—the West Side

The West Side of Chicago has some areas of neat apartments and houses, but much of the area is in need of repair. Many of the West Side's 600,000 residents live in decaying buildings. About 60 percent are black; the rest are white.

City officials are very much aware of the problems they face in this part of town. They know the crime rate is high. They are aware that many of the people are unemployed. Many of the old factories and abandoned warehouses should

Trees and shrubs are common in many Chicago neighborhoods. Many neighborhoods are like small towns that are part of the big city.

be torn down, they know. But so far they haven't done much to help.

Some West Siders are interested in making their neighborhoods better. For better or for worse, they say, the choice is up to them. Rather than wait years for city government to come up with a plan to relieve the overcrowding and poverty, they say, why not make a start themselves? They're beginning to do just that!

Not all the neighborhoods on the West Side are in trouble. South Lawndale and Austin are two neighborhoods that are attractive, neat places. The housing there is old, but it is well taken care of.

THE MAIN ATTRACTIONS

For a visitor, Chicago offers hundreds and hundreds of interesting things to see and do. Many of the activities are inexpensive—more than a few are absolutely free!

One popular stop for sightseers is the famous Buckingham Memorial Fountain—the world's largest lighted fountain. In the summer there is a computer-programmed light show, with a rainbow of water streaming 135 feet into the air!

Lake Michigan and the lakefront are beautiful park areas. One writer remarked that Chicago was one of the few cities that had the good sense

Grant Park, a green oasis between The Loop and Lake Michigan, is the site of a museum, aquarium, planetarium, convention center, and band shell.

to use its lakefront as a "front yard" rather than load it up with docks and boring warehouses. Miles of green parks stretch along the lake. Lincoln Park, Jackson Park, Grant Park—all have lots of space for family fun.

Buckingham Memorial Fountain in Grant Park operates daily during the summer. Colorful lights make the fountain a showpiece each evening.

Wrigley Field is the home of the Chicago Cubs, Chicago's National League baseball team. Chicago's other baseball team, the White Sox, plays in the American League.

A Sporting Town

Chicago is proud of its professional athletes, and there are many of them!

The city has two major league baseball teams. The Chicago White Sox of the American League play their games on the South Side, at Comiskey Park. The Cubs of the National League play on the North Side, at Wrigley Field. Until recently only daytime games could be played at Wrigley Field. Nearby residents of the North Side neighborhood protested that the lights needed for night games would disturb them. In 1988 they finally gave up, and lights were installed.

Chicago's football team is the 1985 Super Bowl Champion Chicago Bears. Fans will confide that the football season lets them forget just how miserable Chicago's baseball season was! The Bears play their games at windy Soldier Field, right next to the lake.

Chicago Stadium is home to both the city's pro hockey and basketball teams. Chicagoans are proud of the Chicago Bulls, led by exciting star Michael Jordan, and the Blackhawks of the National Hockey League.

My Aching Feet!

There are perhaps more kinds of museums in Chicago than in any other city you could name. Exhibits display paintings from around the world, live piranhas devouring smaller fish, Afro-American art, Polish stained glass, and melted marbles from the Chicago Fire. You name it, Chicago has it on display!

A favorite spot for native Chicagoans and visitors alike is the Field Museum of Natural History. In addition to the huge permanent dinosaur displays and lifelike stuffed animals from every continent on earth, the Field Museum has exhibits that

Works of art from around the world are on display in the many halls of the Art Insitute of Chicago.

The Conservatory in Lincoln Park is a popular stop for flower lovers.

change every so often. There are free films, lectures, and activities for children.

Another of the most popular museums is the Museum of Science and Industry. There are 14 acres of exciting displays—many of them "hands-on exhibits." Visitors can walk through a real Nazi U-boat, descend into the eerie blackness of a working coal mine, and take a computerized driving test.

When the lights come on, a walking tour of downtown Chicago is always worthwhile!

★ GOVERNING THE PEOPLE ★

The government of Chicago is made up of a mayor and a city council. The council is made up of 50 aldermen, one from each of the city's 50 wards.

The aldermen and the mayor are elected by the people of Chicago for four-year terms. Some have served many four-year terms. Together, the mayor and the council make most of the decisions about how the city will be run. In addition, there are commissioners appointed by the mayor and approved by the council. These commissioners are responsible for the city's parks, the police, and the fire department, for example.

Chicago is different from many other big cities in that it has what is known as a "weak mayor, strong city council" form of government. That means that the city council has more power than the mayor. The council has the power to make the laws, and the mayor must carry them out.

In many large cities, a mayor can choose assistants or make decisions about issues. In Chicago, however, the mayor must get approval from the city council.

"The City That Works"

It seems odd that a city with a weak mayoral system of government should have produced one of the most powerful mayors in the United States, but it's true.

For 21 years under Mayor Richard J. Daley, Chicago thrived and prospered. Elected in 1955, Daley was also head of the Democratic Party in Cook County, of which Chicago is a part. Between his county post and his job as mayor, Daley was a very powerful man.

Daley prided himself on keeping

As well as housing government offices, the State of Illinois Center is noted for its unusual architecture.

the city strong. He knew that other big cities were having problems, but he intended to keep Chicago on course. Calling Chicago "The City That Works," Daley made sure that city services such as garbage collection, water, and street lights were reliable.

Because of his position in the Cook County Democratic Party, Daley was able to control who held most of the important offices in the state. That enabled him to keep tight control over what went on in Chicago.

As his power grew, politicians realized they needed his support if they were to be successful. Daley could almost guarantee votes to his favorite candidate. That even applied to national elections. After losing the presidential race to John Kennedy in 1960, Richard Nixon blamed his defeat on Daley and his powerful hold on Illinois.

Daley was both loved and despised. Although many blacks were loyal to him, other blacks called him a racist and a bigot. Other politicians accused him of favoritism, putting his friends and family in important city jobs.

Mayor Daley took pride in a city that worked!

Yet his most bitter rivals admitted that Daley's death in 1976 marked the end of one of the most powerful political figures of the 20th century.

After Daley

His successors have had limited success in dealing with Chicago's problems. Jane Byrne was elected in 1979. A former supporter of Daley, she was the first woman to be elected mayor of Chicago.

Byrne was defeated in 1983 by a black Congressman named Harold Washington. Washington had diffi-culties working with the city council, although his supporters believed that his programs would work if given a chance. The fact remained that Washington was unable to gain the support of the aldermen. He hadn't the political might that Daley had had, and the council knew it.

When Washington died unexpectedly of a heart attack in 1987, another black leader, Eugene Sawyer, stepped in as acting mayor. Time will tell if Sawyer and the city council will be able to work together to tackle the problems facing Chicago.

Like the lake along which it grew, Chicago is a city of change and strength.

One of Chicago's most famous writers, Studs Terkel, has compared a Chicagoan walking around the city to a man who has lost many teeth, feeling around his mouth with his tongue. Change is everywhere—it is going on all the time. Like the toothless man, Chicagoans explore those new places, looking for something that feels familiar, but they aren't always successful.

Some cities are hampered by people's fear of change. They don't trust it and they don't like it. But Chicagoans expect change. Buildings and factories are torn down, and

Carl Sandburg's "City of Big Shoulders" is still always moving, always working. Chicago is a city of planning and building and rebuilding.

new structures go up. The city is a crazy-quilt of the old and the new. Brand-new multi-million dollar skyscrapers stand next to elegant buildings over a century old.

Chicago is a strong, powerful city. Chicago's willingness to change and start again might be the most powerful ammunition it has in this modern battle.

Elegant old buildings, such as the Wrigley Building (right) and the Tribune Building, are part of Chicago's heritage. Since the late 1800's, Chicago has been known for its architectural excellence.

*Chicago, Illinois

IMPORTANT FACTS

- Population: 3,009,530 (1986 estimate)
  Rank: 3
- Population of metropolitan area: 6,188,000
  Rank: 3
- Mayor: Eugene Sawyer (acting mayor until next election, April 1991.)
- Seat of Cook County

- Land area: 228.1 sq. miles
- Monthly normal temperature:
  January—21.4°F
  July—73.0°F
- Average annual precipitation: 33.34"
- Latitude: 41° 52' 28" N
- Longitude: 87° 38' 22" W
- Altitude: ranges from 578.5 ft. to 672 ft.

- Time zone: Central

- Annual events:
  St. Patrick's Day Parade, March 17
  International Art Expo, May
  Blues Festival, Grant Park, early June
  Gold Coast Art Fair, August
  Chicago River Festival, August
  International Film Festival, November

IMPORTANT DATES

1673—French-Canadian explorers Joliet and Marquette were first non-Indian visitors to Chicago area.

1770—black fur trader du Sable settled in Chicago area.

1800—settlers from East moved in.

1812—settlers attacked by Potawatomi Indians; Fort Dearborn destroyed.

1816—settlers returned to Chicago area.

1837—Chicago incorporated as city.

1848—shipping canals built, linking Chicago and Mississippi Rivers.

1857—Chicago became railroad center.

1871—Great Chicago Fire left 300 people dead and 100,000 homeless.

1885—first steel-framed skyscraper built in Chicago.

1920's—Prohibition led to increased crime; gangster Al Capone terrorized city.

1955—Richard Daley elected mayor.

1971—Chicago's Union Stockyards closed.

1979—Jane Byrne elected mayor, first woman mayor of Chicago.

1983—Harold Washington elected mayor; died in 1987.

1988—lights installed at Wrigley Field.

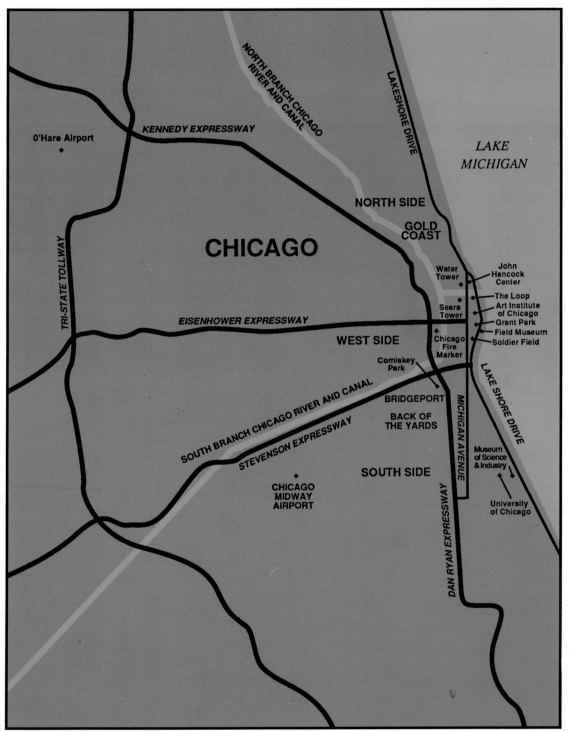

©1989 Mark E. Ahlstrom

Unit District #5 Elementary
Instructional Media Center -2

★ GLOSSARY ★

architect—someone who designs new buildings.

bootlegging—the illegal sale and distribution of liquor, such as happened in the 1920's.

Cabrini-Green—a crime-ridden housing project on Chicago's North Side.

Capone, Al—a gangster who ruled Chicago's crime scene during the 1920's.

Comiskey Park—a baseball stadium on the South Side of Chicago. The White Sox play all their home games at Comiskey Park.

Fort Dearborn—a U.S. military fort built on the site of modern Chicago. The fort was burned in an Indian attack in 1812.

Daley, Richard—mayor of Chicago for 21 years, from 1955 to 1976. Daley was a powerful force in city, state, and national politics.

Du Sable, Jean Baptiste Point—black trader who established the first non-Indian settlement on the site of what is now Chicago, in the 1770's.

Joliet, Louis and Marquette, Jacques—two French explorers who came upon the site of what is now Chicago, in 1673.

Magnificent Mile—part of Michigan Avenue (north of the Loop) that has glamorous shops, hotels, restaurants, and offices.

O'Leary cow—animal blamed for kicking over a lantern and starting the Great Chicago Fire of 1871.

Loop—a section of downtown Chicago so named because of the "loop" of e l e v a t e d train tracks that ring the area.

portage—to carry a canoe from one body of water to another.

Potawatomi—tribe of Native Americans who first inhabited the area that is now Chicago.

Prohibition—a time in the 1920's when it was illegal to drink, sell, or distribute liquor.

rotunda—a curved or circular tower on a building. The Carson's building in Chicago has a rotunda.

Sandburg, Carl—poet who lived in and wrote about Chicago.

Sears Tower—the tallest building in the world.

stockyards—a place where cattle, pigs, and sheep are brought to be butchered and shipped all over the United States. Chicago at one time had the largest stockyards in the country.

Wrigley Field—a baseball stadium on the North Side. The Chicago Cubs play all of their home games at Wrigley Field.

★ INDEX ★